Bow wow!

From the tips of our noses to the tips of our tails, we dogs do funny things. We admit it. We know we make you laugh. But now it's time to understand why! That's the reason we wrote this book. We howl, we dig, we drool, and we bow — but we have lots of different reasons for acting the way we do!

Are you ready to find out WHY we are the way we are?

Why are dogs' noses always wet?

This is an easy question to answer, because it's not true. Our noses are not always wet. They only get wet when we lick them! That makes sense, doesn't it?

Humans say that a wet nose means a dog is healthy. That's not *really* true, either. But there is a reason people believe the story. A happy, healthy dog usually licks its nose a lot. So a healthy dog often has a wet nose! A dog that isn't feeling well won't lick its nose as much.

So there you are! You can't always believe what you smell — that is, hear!

Most Likely to Be Wet

And the winner is . . .

Poodles! Did you ever notice how much Poodle sounds like *puddle*? The name Poodle actually came from the German word *pudel*, which means "one who plays in water."

Honorable Mention:
Labrador Retriever — and not just its nose! Labs are happiest when they're running into the water. They like to bring back something special for their best friend.

Why do dogs sniff EVERYTHING?

Isn't it more fun to do the things you do well than the things you don't? Well, dogs do an excellent job of sniffing. So we do it a lot! In fact, we don't want to brag, but we're much better sniffers than humans are.

Dogs have about 220 million cells for smelling. A human being only has about 5 million.

A good sense of smell helps us dogs find out what's going on in the world. It tells us where we are. It tells us who has been there before us. We can find out if danger is near or if food is close by. Whatever there is to find out, we can find it out through smell.

Our sense of smell is why a lot of dogs have jobs. It means we can be very good as law enforcement helpers.

Most Nosy

And the winner is . . .

Even though wolves don't make very good pets, they're a kind of wild dog. A wolf can smell a deer from 1½ miles away! And they can hear a howl from 4 miles away.

Tails of Courage

Have you ever heard of the great sled dog named Balto? In 1925, Balto was the lead dog of the final sled team that delivered antitoxin serum to Nome, Alaska. He saved the children of Nome from a diptheria epidemic. Now *there's* a leader of the pack!

We understand that drooling can seem gross to you. It's a little gross to some of us, too. (We don't all do it!) But we want to defend those dogs that drool. It's really not their fault. It happens because they have loose skin around their jaws and mouths.

Dogs like Basset Hounds, Bullmastiffs, and Saint Bernards are some of the biggest droolers. When they start exercising or eating, their saliva glands get going (just like yours do). They can't stop them.

Gives another meaning to that phrase "Loose lips sink ships," don't you think?

HEALTH WATCH

If your dog suddenly starts to drool but has no history of drooling, it could mean that something is wrong. It's a good time to check in with your vet!

Biggest Eater

And the winner is . . .

Siberian Husky sled dogs! Boy, oh boy, can those dogs eat! Most dogs eat about 1,500 calories a day. A sled dog eats between 10,000 and 14,000! "Chow" do you like that?!

Why do dogs howl at the moon?

If you could call all your friends at once, would you do it?

You wouldn't have to use a phone, and the call would be free. You could talk to everyone at once.

Pretty neat, huh? Well, that's what howling is for us dogs. It's our way of saying, "Hey! Is there anybody out there who is part of my pack? Please meet me here under the moon at twelve o'clock sharp! I'll be waiting!"

Of course, some of us howl just because we enjoy singing!

P.S. We're not really howling at the moon. Howling just works better when your head is bent back in that position, so it only *looks* like we're howling up at the moon.

Least Likely to Howl

And the winner is . . .

The Basenji! Poor thing. This African wolf dog is the only dog in the world that can't bark at all! What do you have to say about that? (More than the Basenji, we bet!)

All in the Family

There's no rule that says a pack has to be made up of dogs only. Check out an amazing story called *The Incredible Journey*. It's about a **Bull Terrier**, a **Labrador Retriever**, and a Siamese **CAT**. These three friends walked more than 200 miles over the Rocky Mountains to find their family!

Why do dogs wiggle their ears so much?

Ears are a very important part of communication. They do a lot more than just listen. We dogs use our ears to talk, too.

Dogs who are listening intently will probably stick their ears straight up. We tend to do this when we hear the word "walk" or "bone."

Dogs who want to say, "I'm NOT in charge," will probably drop their ears down.

This isn't much different from human beings. If you had a tail and if your ears looked as good as ours, you'd probably move them around just like we do!

Biggest Ears

And the winner is . . .

The Basset Hound . . . paws down! Or, in this case — ears down! One of the biggest problems a Basset Hound has is trying not to step on its own ears. Have you ever *heard* of such a thing!?

How do dogs hear whistles that don't make a sound?

You might not think a dog whistle makes noise, but we think they sound like the inside of a tuba! That's because dogs hear a much wider range of sound than humans do.

We don't want to brag about our hearing, but a fact is a fact. Sound pitch is measured by units called *Hertz*. Dogs hear all the way up into the 100,000 Hertz range, while people can only hear in the 16,000–20,000 Hertz range.

Sorry, but you know what they say. The truth "hertz"!

Most Likely to Succeed

And the winner is . . .

It's a dog-eat-dog world out there. You need brains to make it! That's why we're giving this award to the smartest dogs we know: the Australian Shepherd, the Collie, the Poodle, and the Doberman Pinscher!

Lost and Hound
Did you know a **Saint Bernard** can rescue people buried deep in the snow? One of the most famous **Saint Bernards** was named Barry. Between 1800 and 1810, he saved more than 40 people trapped in the snow!

Why do dogs bow down on their front legs?

If you saw a dog with its front legs extended, chest on the ground, back end in the air, ears back, tail up and wagging, and mouth yap-yap-yapping, what would you do?

A.   Run away and climb a tree.
B.   Give the dog some food.
C.   Grab a ball and start to play.
D.   Bow back to the dog.

The answer is C! All these actions say, "Let's play!" We use body language to make our point. The next time you see a dog doing these things, look for the nearest stick and throw it!

Most Playful

And the winner is . . .

The Cairn Terrier! This dog knows how to have fun . . . and how to bark, too! You might call it noisy. We call it playful.

# Why do dogs dig?

Why do we dig? Because it's really, really fun!
And it's our job.

We can give you a bunch of great reasons to dig.

1. COOLING SYSTEM

   Ever lay in a brand-new hole on a really hot day?
   It's the best feeling in the world.

2. HUNTING

   Ever race a mole to the end of its hole? It's a lot of
   fun and it takes some fast digging!

3. ESCAPE

   Ever try to jump over a 6-foot fence? It's a lot
   easier to go under than over!

4. BURYING THINGS

   Ever try to bury something without digging? It's
   kind of impossible!

5. EXERCISE

   Ever do 20 minutes of serious digging? It'll build
   up some strong muscles!

Most Likely to Dig to China

And the winner is . . .

We split the award. Any dog with the word Terrier in its name is a winner. Terriers are super diggers!

 Why do dogs bury bones?

Why did you put the other half of your tuna-fish sandwich in the fridge for later? Probably for some of the same reasons we bury things.

In the old days, we dogs ran wild and free. We had to hunt and kill our food. We often killed things that were too big to eat all at once. If we had had wings, we could have flown our leftovers up into a tree. Or if we had had refrigerators, we might have tried saving them the way you do. But we didn't.

That's why we buried our leftovers, so we could come back for them later. Otherwise, the hyenas or vultures or other animals would have stolen our food!

Least Likely to Share Leftovers

And the winner is . . .

We can't agree on a winner. Just like people, lots of dogs can be moody sometimes!

Buried Treasures

Did you hear about the man who took his dog for a walk on the beach and found a 550,000-year-old ax? It's possibly the oldest man-made object ever found in northern Europe. Dig it!

Why do dogs fetch?

Not every dog *does* fetch. Most dogs are *taught* to fetch. There are some natural fetchers, such as Labs, Retrievers, and Border Collies. But a lot of us dogs don't want to bring something back once we have it.

Border Collies learn to "fetch" sheep for their farmers. They go after sheep that wander away from the herd. These dogs know how to round up livestock.

Now *that's* fetching!

Teacher's Pet

And the winner is . . .

The Golden Retriever. This dog has beauty *and* brains. It's also dependable, loving, and playful — and it doesn't ruin the furniture.

Why do dogs roll over on their backs?

It's important to know who is the boss. We dogs have figured out how to make that fact really clear. Whenever we get together, we get the word out fast. We do it in lots of ways.

A dog that rolls onto its back knows he or she is definitely *not* in charge!

If a dog is trying to say, "I'm not going to make any trouble! You're the boss, not me!" the key word is *DOWN.*

Keep your eyes down.
Keep your tail down (and between your legs).
Keep your ears down.

You could also try face-licking, if all else fails.

Sweetest

And the winner is . . .

This is another tough choice. We're *all* friendly, after all! But we agree the Beagle is one of the sweetest dogs around, even if they might cause a little trouble here and there!

Why do dogs shed?

Most people think shedding has to do with hot and cold weather. The truth is, light tells us dogs when to shed. The more light there is (like during longer, sunnier days in the summer), the more we'll shed.

Every dog sheds. Some do it more than others. It never hurts to help us out with a good brush. Not only will we look nice, but regular brushing will keep our fur and skin in better shape.

HEALTH WATCH

Dogs might start shedding if they are sick, stressed, or pregnant. So don't ignore it if your dog starts shedding more than usual!

Best Fur

And the winner is . . .

The Afghan Hound! This dog has some pretty soft, good-looking fur!

Why do dogs get so excited when they see other dogs?

We think this is a silly question. What could be more exciting than seeing another dog like us? We dogs are pack-crazy! We love to run with a crowd of creatures just like ourselves.

But it's not as messy as it looks. We sometimes pick a leader, so that everyone knows who's in charge. We usually decide who is in charge after a lot of sniffing. That's why it's so important to get close to another dog when we see one. It's hard to do a complete job of sniffing if you aren't allowed to get good and close!

Most Likely to Be Leader of the Pack

And the winner is . . .

We think it's only fair to award this honor twice. So we're giving it to the little Chihuahua and the big Doberman Pinscher. As Mark Twain said, "It's not the size of the dog in the fight, it's the size of the fight in the dog."

Why do dogs wag their tails?

Our tails are pretty important. If we wag our tail loosely, it's a good way to say:

"Hey! How are you? Good to see you! Wanna play? Do you have a ball? Wouldn't it be fun to play with a ball? Did I say hello? Hi! Hello! How do you do?"

But you also might see one of us with our tail hanging low. We're probably saying:

"I think you're cool, dude. You're bigger. You're stronger. I'm not going to bother you."

Happiest Tail-Wagger

And the winner is . . .

The Irish Setter! And why not? They're beautiful, playful, and smart!

Honorable Mention:

The Brittany . . . as long as nobody docks* its tail.

* *Dock* means "cut short."

What kind of funny dog would you like to have?

Which breeds are a good match for you and your family? Ask yourself these questions: *Where do you live? How much space do you have for a dog? Do you have a yard? Do you have other animals in your house? How much time can you spend with a dog?*

After you decide which breeds (or mixes of breeds) are good matches, you need to meet some actual dogs. There are lots of dogs waiting to be adopted!

Dogs and people have a lot in common. Each of us acts funny in our own special way! So, just as you must get to know your human friends, you need to get to know a dog!

We, the dogs, promise there is a perfect dog out there for you. You just have to find it.

Good Luck . . . or, as we like to say, *WOOF!*